Never Too Late

Selected Poems and New

T. M. Moore

RESOURCE *Publications* · Eugene, Oregon

NEVER TOO LATE
Selected Poems and New

Wipf & Stock
An Imprint of Wipf and Stock Publishers
199 W. 8th Ave., Suite 3
Eugene, OR 97401

www.wipfandstock.com

PAPERBACK ISBN: 979-8-3852-4626-7
HARDCOVER ISBN: 979-8-3852-4627-4
EBOOK ISBN: 979-8-3852-4628-1

"Each poem in this collection aims to 'rout / confusion,' to pull up weeds of vice or folly and till the ground for praise, illumination, and virtue. As a result, T. M. Moore has given us words that can be lived by amid darkness both existential and quotidian."
—Jeffrey Bilbro, Associate Professor of English Literature, Grove City College

"Soaked in Scripture and biblical wisdom, T. M. Moore's marvelous collection of poetry will delight you; the variety of forms, meter, and moods he employs. Some tickle the ears, others place us in front of a mirror, and still others force us to contemplate eternity. But more importantly, T. M.'s poetry begs us, compels us, to open our eyes! To see the hand of God in the world around us, and to embrace every moment as a gift from our Creator and an opportunity to bring him glory in the smallest of tasks or greatest of challenges."
—David Carlson, Retired Editor, *BreakPoint* with Chuck Colson

"From the whisper of thunder, to Susie's bridge, to the call of the leaf, these rare poetic jewels take us through all the vicissitudes of life, both its joys and its sorrows. These lovely words deserve slow, meditative consumption in order to change not only one's point of view but one's very character. Our age is in desperate need of good poetry even though it may not know it. *Never Too Late* by the incomparable T. M. Moore is a good place to start."
—William Edgar, Professor Emeritus of Apologetics, Westminster Theological Seminary, Philadelphia

"T. M. Moore has an unparalleled ability to write poetry that is completely natural and unforced while maintaining the enchantment of rhyme and meter. I think Shakespeare would have envied him. And too, like Shakespeare, within the beautiful lines is real substance that transcends any ideology and

communicates direct truths of the universe capable of connecting with the human spirit, or at least the human poet."
—Evan Mantyk, President, The Society of Classical Poets, Mount Hope, New York

"In *Never Too Late*, T. M. Moore reminds us that God speaks to us through all seasons and activities of life. Through the power of poetical insight, Moore explores the wonders of creation, the mystery of marriage, the shadow of death, and our longing for Christ's Kingdom to come. These pages contain a lifetime of wisdom, filtered through the Scriptures and distilled to their most potent essence through the discipline of poetry."
—M. G. Moland, Dean of Education, Arts and Sciences, LeTourneau University

Contents

Foreword   9

Part 1: The Power to Advantage   11

    The Deep Springs of My Soul   13
    The Blank Page   14
    Let Me   15
    A Curious Contingency   17
    Let Not My Words   18
    Breeze Borne   19
    Poetry   20
    In Two Minds   21
    Subject Matter   22
    Raison D'être   23
    The Spark of Art and Spirit   24
    Jack-in-the-Box   25
    Brick Maker   26
    Fault Lines   27
    A Plethora of Poems   28
    Pollinator   29
    Love of Craft   30

Part 2: Love in the Everyday   31

    Cup of Daisies   33
    My World   34
    Life Bread   35
    Reflections   36
    She Lay Beside Me   37
    Bridge   38
    Enough!   38
    Baking Day   39

Desuetude   40
But a Thread   41
Anniversary   42
Gift   42
Gray   43

Part 3: Word Beyond Words   45

Common Things   47
Ambassadors of Glory   48
My Powers of Observation   49
Centaury   50
A Ceaseless Flow   51
Photons of Thought   52
The Little Things   53
Defiant   54
When Snow Falls   55
Frail Saplings   57
Just Doin' Our Job   58
Logos   59
Slow Reviving   60
Whisper of Thunder   61
The Ruin of My Sin   62
Common Brief   63

Part 4: On Earth as in Heaven   65

I Heard the Sound of Armies   67
Curve   68
Faith   69
Meditations While Reading Ephrem the Syrian
        Meditation 1   70
        Meditation 2   71
        Meditation 3   73

Meditation 4   75
Meditation 5   76
Palimpsest   77
The Coming of the Kingdom   78
Trees in Winter   79
Wear Smooth My Rungs   80
What Job Came to Understand   81

Part 5: Mind Training   83

The Art of Life   85
Ray of Dawn   86
Looking Up   94
Music to Part the Veil   98

Part 6: Remaining Time   103

The Mourners   105
The Dying   106
Years of Strength   107
Hourglass   108
Tents   109
Above All Regrets   110
And When I Die   111
April Snow   112
Never Too Late   113
Offering   114

Acknowledgements   115

For Susie

Foreword

Jonathan Edwards wrote that time is a most precious gift of God. He's right, of course, because everything we do, we do in time. Without time, that continuous succession of moments coming to us by the grace of God, we would be able to do nothing. We would not exist.

Close to time among the innumerable gifts of God are words. Words fill up a good bit of our time. These days our words tend to be mostly practical. We use them as we need them without too much care about how they sound or whether our use of words might be improved. Sort of like the way we use our time. But words are a gift of God and, as with all gifts of God, they should be used for His glory and the edification of those around us.

Poetry can highlight the wonder and power of words. Reading poetry—especially formal poetry—can help us learn to appreciate the ordinary beauty of our ordinary words, in the ordinary time of our lives. It does this by leading us to slow down, hear and savor words, delight in their sounds and senses, and listen as the words speak to and against and on behalf of one another. Poetry is a way to enhance our stewardship of words.

It's a tall order, but poetry is up to it. And our hope—Susie and mine—is that taking the time to ponder this little collection of verses might enrich your appreciation for words and the things they delineate or define.

The poems in this volume are arranged in six parts. Part 1 offers a kind of justification for this project: Why would anyone want to write poetry? Or write anything?

Part 2 considers ways that my wife Susie expresses the love she has for God and life and, happily, for me.

Part 3 exercises our skills in seeing the glory of God in the works of His hands, especially in the creation that surrounds us everywhere.

Part 4 addresses living in a world where unseen realities and spiritual striving must not be overlooked, as they are inescapable and rightly interfacing with them is essential.

In Part 5 I invite you to consider three stories in the form of verse essays. These poems are somewhat longer, but this will give readers the opportunity to observe words at work in extended and subtle ways.

Finally, Part 6 invites us to face up to the inevitable with hope. And as we do, to make sure that we do not waste the opportunities granted each day to know full and abundant life in Jesus Christ.

My wife, Susie, edits and improves all my writing, including my poetry. I'm grateful for her support, encouragement, and assistance. We pray that the poems in this volume will encourage you in your use of the gift of words. It's never too late, whatever the time of your life, to make better use of all the gifts of God.

T. M. Moore
Essex Junction, VT

Part 1: The Power to Advantage

Words and Writing

Other pleasures fail us, or wound us while they charm; but the pen we take up with rejoicing and lay down with satisfaction, for it has the power to advantage not only its lord and master, but many others as well, even though they be far away—sometimes, indeed, even though they be not born for thousands of years to come.

Petrarch (*Letters*)

The Deep Springs of My Soul
Job 32.18-22

For I am full of words! The Spirit in
me seeks expression and compels me to
disperse my thoughts to anybody who
will read them with approval or chagrin.

I write because I must. It's my intent
to steward wisely all my words, to do
some lasting work that may move others to
rejoice, rethink, refocus, or repent.

Each day, as I release fresh words within
my sphere, my guiding aim is: All things true
and excellent for bringing glory to
our God, Whose lasting favor I would win.

Release the deep springs of my soul, O Lord,
and draw forth, sanctified, each single word.

The Blank Page

The blank page calls, just like your mother when
she called you home for dinner, standing on
the front porch, not quite certain where you were,
but knowing you'd be somewhere you could hear
her voice. You might be roaming with some friends
around the neighborhood or playing in
the weed-filled field across the street, or up
the elm tree in the front yard. She would call
but once. You knew the rule: Come when you're called.
As dinner time approached all other sounds
receded or were somehow magically
suppressed so you'd be sure to hear her when
she called. To fail meant missing dinner and
perhaps a consequence more dire still.

So keep your ear cocked, and don't stray too far
or let yourself become so occupied
with other things that you do not respond
according to the rule each time the blank
page calls to summon, from whatever niche
or hiding place, the unseen words it seeks.

Let Me

Here sits the busy writer, glimpsed, not all
that long ago, within the longings of
a busy pastor as a vision small,

unlikely, but desired by him above
his then vocation. Often, pondering such
a prospect, he'd reflect how much he'd love

that calling, that he'd find it to be much
more suited to his skills and interests, more
the kind of work to let him get in touch

with who he really is and what's in store
for him in the divine economy.
How many times did he with tears implore

the Lord for just this opportunity!
Now here he sits, by deadlines harried to
distraction, writing projects yet to be

completed, just in time for more to do.
He's gazing out the window of his mind
and conjuring a vision fresh and new

of him unhurried, laboring to find
the proper form, the trope, the right device
to set the burdens of his aching mind

into poetic works of art. Ah, yes!
The unrushed leisure of the poet! Let
me take up that vocation, Lord, and bless

me with some quiet in my soul! Forget
about these deadlines; lavish me with time
to think, with books and friends to help me set

my mind on matters holy and sublime!
Let me befriend more of the creatures of
Your world, and by their witness, let me climb

new heights of glory, where you dwell above,
that I may know more of Your steadfast love!

A Curious Contingency

The modern order is largely a product of contingency.
Stephen Jay Gould

The fruits of my vocation blossom from
a kind of cosmic soup of latent power:
books, note cards, memos, shreds and shards of some
fresh-excavated pile or file; an hour
on this, an hour on that—the only plan
a loose and highly opportunistic scheme,
a kind of curious contingency more than
a plan: so my haphazard style must seem
to some—things finished, in the works, or just
not ever put away, the sediment
of labors past now buried beneath the dust
of new endeavors. An unlikely bent
for one whose work insists on forms, designs,
and arguments tight as a sonnet's lines.

Let Not My Words
1 Samuel 3.19

Let not my words fall to the ground, O Lord,
like Onan's wasted, self-indulgent seed.
Let my words sound Your ever-fruitful Word,

and let them be far-flung, and gladly heard
or read according to each person's need.
Let not my words fall to the ground, O Lord,

like some old, splintered, poorly-fastened board.
Let many build with them, and as they read,
let my words sound your ever-fruitful Word.

And in the chambers of men's souls, deep bored,
let them embed and germinate with speed.
Let not my words fall to the ground, O Lord,

but draw them from Your scabbard with Your Sword,
and let them truth advance and lies impede,
that they may sound Your ever-fruitful Word.

Let my vocation with Your will accord,
in diligence and faithfulness, I plead.
Let not my words fall to the ground, O Lord;
but let them sound Your ever-fruitful Word.

Breeze Borne

I'm meditating, deep in reverie
and thought. Ideas are drifting in and out;
some settle, then connect and join to be

a point of view, an argument about
some matter of importance. I should write
this down. I grab a pen (it's how I rout

confusion) when a feeling of delight
engulfs me, cued up by the window blind
that shimmers in the passing breeze. And right

away the vision forming in my mind
is heightened, clarified, as though the chaff
has blown away, allowing me to find

the kernel I am seeking. And I laugh
out loud and write another paragraph.

Poetry

Am I alone in this? A subtle stirring
within my chest will quicken any time
I come across the word. It's like some prime
condition in my soul, both reassuring
and troubling, like a tiny kitten purring,
a lion pacing, or some life from slime
emerging, seeking beauty. And then I'm
on high alert, lights flashing, systems whirring.

Say "poetry," or any cognate of
it—"poem," "poetic"; mention any poet
I know and whose work I have come to love,
or quote some well-wrought lines: before you know it,
I'm interrupted, as if from Above,
and searching for some seed, and how to sow it.

In Two Minds

Οὐκ οἶδ᾽ ὄττι θέω, δύο μοι τὰ νοήματα
Sappho

That Sapphic fragment is a window to
the soul: "I know not what to do; two minds
exist within me." Everybody finds
themselves here, unsure what to do
or how to choose between two options. You
know what she means. Confronting different kinds
of choices and decisions often blinds
us to the obvious path, the right and true:
Whatever aggrandizes self at the
expense of others, chooses chaos more
than order, mere expression without beauty,
or despair instead of hope, just cannot be
right thinking. Faced with some uncertain door,
enfold yourself in truth. Then do your duty.

Subject Matter

The want of subject matter for my verse
is of my irritants perhaps the worst.

It frequently occurs that I will find
myself without a topic. Wrack my mind,

thumb through my notebooks, close my eyes and try
to see into the images that lie

within my brain—when none of these produce
a subject, I might say, "Oh, what's the use?"

and turn to less demanding projects. Such
times are to be expected, not so much

because there really isn't anything
to write about, but mainly that I bring

to this endeavor such imperfect skill,
and take but little time to train my will

to find, examine, and consider ways
to make quotidian incidentals praise

the God Whose glory in them shines. But let
me sense God calling to me and I'll set

my heart and mind to draw, from everyday
occurrences and things, the drift and sway

of other-worldly Presences. And then
verse may announce itself to me again.

Raison D'être

What is this little poem of mine?
A cast of words and meter, line
and rhyme; a thought, a soaring hope,
me clinging to life-saving rope;
a gesture made to no one, to
the world, to anybody who,
deep in his soul, aspires to more.
These simple lines in feet of four
and strict end-line agreement may
not change the world or save the day;
they won't be read or memorized
by kids in school (I should have prized
those exercises more). These words
will huddle here, I guess, like birds
perched on a wire, which, just because
they're ordinary, few will pause
to contemplate how beautiful
they are just being there. The pull
or push of something in my soul
demands that I mark up my scroll
from time to time with musings such
as this. It's how I get in touch
with my small world and self, and nod
with thanks to the eternal God
for things like rhythm, sound, delight,
and simple words to think and write.

The Spark of Art and Spirit

First day of class: The lies begin,
as students everywhere embark
upon their path of self-deceit.

Condemned to droning lectures, thin
with truth, they take their notes and mark
their textbooks, that they may repeat

the sought-for information in
exams when called upon to bark
for their degrees—a process neat

and smooth, by which they hope to win
a cubicle, a space to park,
adoring lovers, and complete,

unbridled freedom. Truth is spin
and life is lust without the spark
of art and Spirit. Time will beat

them finally as, to their chagrin,
their youthful day fades fast to dark
and nothing but the end will meet

them. Thus, the sickness that sets in
while they're preparing for the lark
they hope their lives will be, will cheat

them of their souls, and they'll grow thin
within, decrepit, wretched, stark
exemplars of an age replete

with things but having nothing. Sweet
the antidote, would they but eat.

Jack-in-the-Box

The pleasure in the thing is, first, the way
it *looks*. A form that one can recognize,
that captivates, attracts, and holds the eyes,
is much more likely to result in play
than one that's merely random, shall we say.
There follows next the *feel*, as one applies
himself to handling it, and as he tries
the crank. The *music* that ensues should sway
within the soul and make his hand obey
the sweet momentum that each plunge and rise
creates. Anticipation builds, like skies
with thunder rumbling on a summer's day.
So turn it slowly, hold your breath and wait—
he's in there; he won't tarry or be late.

Brick Maker

What's that I'm making? Bricks, and nothing more.
These sentences and words are all I know.
I hope their usefulness might long endure.

Don't get me wrong: I love my bricks. I pour
my heart and mind into each one, although
they're only bricks—just bricks, and nothing more.

No soaring edifice or tome's in store
for me. My calling is to bricks, just so.
I hope their usefulness might long endure.

Someone might use my bricks to build a more
impressive structure. Someone else might throw
these bricks I'm making (bricks, and nothing more),

to smash the false front of some worldview store.
I cannot know to what ends they might go;
I hope their usefulness might long endure.

Take these my bricks and set them true and sure;
build beauty with them, or bring hubris low:
I'll keep on making bricks, and nothing more,
and hope their usefulness might long endure.

Fault Lines

Deep, hidden in the earth, extensive, great,
unreconciling pressures meet and grind
against each other, like the two-lobed mind
of some poor tortured poet. The awful weight
of countervailing forces breaks the hold
of friction; vast tectonic plates adjust
to one another in a desperate lust
for primacy of place. The fragile mold
of earth is shaken as the energy
released spreads out in all directions, and
throws into turmoil people, buildings, land
and every pretense of security.
Beware the tremors, therefore; fear the worst,
to tread the fault lines of a poet's verse.

A Plethora of Poems

We need a plethora of poems, a great
monsoon of metaphors, a rainstorm of
new rhymes and rhythms, and a cohort of
creators who have heard God's call to verse
and are responding faithfully to feed
a long-neglected need in every soul.

And may they, like Elijah, stretch themselves
across the body of believers, dead
to verse, and, by the breath of their new songs
unto the Lord, whisper a calling to
the Church, and breathe new life into our souls.

Pollinator

When swift spring breezes suddenly excite
the conifers out back, they really come
alive in dips and bows and surges right
before my eyes. I watch to see if from
a few of them, or even one, a cloud
will be released, all green and dense and fraught
with life. It happens, and I laugh out loud.
It's always grander than I might have thought.

The healthy trees have done their job. Now they
will start all over once again. They know
their place, their purpose, and their powers. They live
to pollinate, and send their gifts away,
not knowing whether anything will grow
from what they lavishly and freely give.

Love of Craft

A conversation between Beauty and Productivity

"You don't have time for this, you know." "Says who?"
"That daily checklist down there in your tool
bar, that's who says!" "Calm down. You need to cool
your jets and let me think." "Think? That's what you
call this? You look more like a water bird,
all hesitation-stepping after some
small morsel." "It's surprising this should come
from you" "That what should come from me?" "You
heard
yourself, I'm sure. That lovely image of
a heron, as I see it?" "That was just
a way of speaking. Look, you really must
get to your work and stop this stuff 'you love.'"
"This 'unproductive stuff', you mean? That drew
that most delightful metaphor from you?"

Part 2: Love in the Ordinary

Two Made One

For love, all love of other sights controls,
And makes one little room an everywhere.

John Donne ("The Good Morrow")

Cup of Daisies

This cup has served us all our one-flesh years.
It bears the nicks and superficial cracks
which come with wear and tear, and while it lacks
the sheen it once possessed, still it appears
and is as solid as it was the day
we said, "I do." These daisies, by your hand
selected, trimmed, arranged, and made to stand
here, radiant like the new day's sunrise, say
to one and all that beauty does not mourn
the passing of the years, but faithfulness,
in spite of wear, makes love to thrive and bless
this happy union, as each day is born.
The daisies wilt, the cup may one day break.
Love tried and solid will new beauties make.

My World

My friends who travel love it, mostly. And
they really get around: To Iceland, France,
the tropics, Patagonia, Disneyland,

the beach, the Outerbanks—the Holy Land's
a favorite—Germany, or Istanbul,
the nation's parks, or Sanabel. No chance

I'm ever going to see those places. Dull,
my life? Not for a moment. All the wide
world and its glories, fascinations full

and wondrous, treats and treasures *bona fide*
and bounteous—all I ever hope to see—
are in this little room, right by my side,

where nightly, I am quite content to be
here in this chair, you sitting next to me.

Life Bread

Χριστοῦ εὐωδία

It reaches me at last, that subtle but
distinct aroma, which, like new life, has
escaped its incubator to diffuse
throughout the house. Yeast mixed with certain kinds
of flour, all the ingredients combined
beneath the maker's strength, set in a shroud
of parchment in a casket, lifeless, cold
and left in darkness. Then, subjected to
the right amount of heat for just the right
amount of time, transformed and made alive,
a gift of grace to nurture life and bring
delight and satisfaction on the wings
of love by the aroma even now
pervading—foretaste of the Bread of life.

Reflections
At the Brandywine River Museum

Behind your beaming, smiling face
the window opened on the creek
at this my favorite earthly place

reflects the slightest shimmering peek
of me adoring you. I stand,
and as I do my knees go weak,

and trembling overtakes my hand,
your elegance and grace to see.
And once again I understand

that I the most blessed man must be
that you reflect such love for me.

She Lay Beside Me

Worn out and weary, feeling out of sorts,
a full day's work before her still, she seemed
as though she'd had enough. Perhaps she dreamed
of places far away, of plush resorts
where others did her bidding, cleaned her room,
and went to market for her; where she could,
uninterruptedly, enjoy a good
night's sleep, like in an undiscovered tomb;
where some all-knowing guru might provide
the key to her malaise, and give her just
the course of action that, if followed, must
allay her woes like the receding tide.
Those lacking, much to my surprise and glee,
she wandered in and snuggled up by me.

Bridge
For Susie, on our 48th Anniversary

No matter if the current of
our lives is peaceable and clear
or swift and troubled, littered here
and there with challenges to love.
One thing together we have proved:
From this Bridge we will not be moved.

Enough!

"Enough!" and out she goes, sun hat pulled low,
short sleeves to dare whatever lingering chill
might try to thwart her springtime-conjuring will.
Yard tools in hand, she heads to where the snow
lay two feet deep two weeks ago. You know
this girl means business. Everything is still
some shade of brown. But nothing here can kill
her firm resolve that winter needs to go,
and go today. And that it should be so,
she tends her gardens, each one looking ill,
though living, cutting back and raking 'til
cruel winter's blast is gone, so things can grow.
The songbirds gather in the trees and sing,
while Susie makes the beds and wakens spring.

Baking Day

Behind me, sounds of baking stir from in
the kitchen. A concerto in three parts
is on the program, as the tuning starts
and instruments appear: a baking tin,
bowls, spoons, whisk, mixer, and a sheet of thin
brown parchment paper (just to keep the tarts
from sticking). The ingredients these arts
require arrive and take their places in
the orchestra. She's ready to begin.
The maestro brings together all the parts:
eggs, milk, three flours, some spices—each imparts
its special contribution, its own spin.
The concert ends in "Bravo!" and "Encore!"
for sweet tarts, scones, and muffins by the score.

Desuetude

On deferring to my editor

I wonder why good words, precise words, fall
into disuse. Too difficult to say?
Or to remember how to spell? Are they
the victims of our laziness? Our small
minds? Or do we who want to use them lack
the fortitude to risk the smirk, the "What?",
or the red pen insisting they be cut
and substituted for? But if they pack
the meaning we intend, then should we not
defend our choice of words, insist on their
propriety and excellence, and dare
the readers to discover a new thought?
But then, the writer's task—it may sound crude—
is to avoid the fate of desuetude.

But a Thread

The cables of suspension bridges stand
as testimony to the genius and
technology of men. Each mighty length
derives its beauty and peculiar strength
from lesser cables, wound together to
comprise the greater strands of steel which do
the heavy lifting, bearing any weight
of buses, cars, and trucks and all their freight
without the slightest strain, complaint, or groan.
In turn, these lesser cables gain their own
integrity from smaller cables still,
of purest steel combined in one strong will.
Take all such cables, bind them strong and true:
They're but a thread in all my love for you.

Anniversary

What is an anniversary? A date
in time. A moment to commemorate
a day of some significance to some
of us, at least. A vantage point wherefrom
to orient and understand events
of lesser import. Lens through which the dense
confusion of our lives falls into place.
The evidence, each passing year, that grace
is real and love is true, that two made one
is where the miracle of love is done
for better, poorer, richer, worse, in health
or sickness, poverty or untold wealth.
Each anniversary gives impulse to
the hope of many more such days with you.

Gift

Wise, patient, knowing, kind, unfazed, content,
sophisticated, pure, intelligent—
like silver, diamond, gold, or rarest wine,
but much more beautiful, and wholly mine—
the greatest gift from heaven's bounty sent.

Gray

I feel a certain loyalty to gray.
Gray days, gray sweaters, cars—gray everything.
Gray soothes and calms. It doesn't boast, or fling
itself before you like some shades do (they
know who they are). Gray broods, as if to say,
"Let's wait and see. Don't get excited, sing
the blues, or dance a jig. Just chill." The thing
is, gray is faithful, always there—no way
gray ever lets you down. Gray won't display,
as if to seek attention. Gray will bring
out other colors, let them show their zing
and fleeting flair, so they can have their day.
But mostly, gray adorns the tresses of
the graycious lady who owns all my love.

Part 3: Word Beyond Words

The Witness of Creation

Those who devote themselves to letters and a life of contemplation, should do so with but one object in view, namely, that they may see in everything the power, the wisdom, and the goodness of God, that they may be filled with love for Him, and may unite themselves so fast to Him in love that they can never be torn away.

Comenius (*The Great Didactic*)

Common Things

You never, Heraclitus claimed,
step in the same stream twice.
Appearances may seem the same
(familiarity's to blame,
or each thing's never-changing name),
but heed that Greek's advice.

There's more to life than meets the eye
or dances on the ear.
The moments of our lives flow by,
fraught with potential we might try;
yet, deaf to their sweet siren cry,
we neither see nor hear.

But hidden in each common thing
and every routine sound,
in leafless trees, on flashing wing,
the songs that common sparrows sing,
and each arriving email's "Ding!"
are wonders to be found.

Step forth, then, into unseen worlds
where mysteries abound.
Eternal truths will be unfurled,
and nagging doubts behind you hurled
when your poor soul is slowly swirled,
turned upright and around
in common things profound.

Ambassadors of Glory
Psalm 19.1-6

They're speaking to us. All created things
ambassadors of glory are to ears
indifferent to their glad reports. The spears
and arrows which commercial culture slings
against us deafen us. Their siren stings
and stabs distort our hearing. Business sears
our eager eardrums; entertainment blears
audition with the piper's tunes it sings.
The echo of banality so rings
within us, hardly anybody hears
creation's message. Whether joy or tears,
we take scant notice of the word it brings.
Throw up a shield around my ears, O Lord,
and let me hear creation's glorious word!

My Powers of Observation

My powers of observation are not what
they ought to be. For revelations swarm
about me! Glory weighs down on me, but
I take scant notice, sound no glad alarm.
There's plenty here to mesmerize and charm
my soul and fill my mind with heavenly thought.
Yet, though it bears down on me like a storm,
I scarcely see it; I will not be taught.
My senses, trained to vanity and what
is merely trite, do not by nature warm
to things sublime, transcendent, perfect. But
God keeps on tugging, tugging at my arm.
Jerk, jostle, jar, cajole, and jolt me, Lord,
and make me see Your all-around-me word.

Centaury

The clear night sky spreads wide a tapestry
of beauty in the stars that shimmer all
throughout the cosmic exhibition hall.
In every age mankind has looked to see
and wonder at the might and mystery
to be discovered there. Wrapped in the thrall
of such majestic beauty, we feel small,
while our thoughts contemplate divinity.

Not all stars occupy the heavens, though.
In sandy, semi-shaded places, right
beneath our feet, bright stars of reddish pink,
a small sun shimmering from their center, wink
and wave and call out to insist the night
sky's beauty matches well with things below.

A Ceaseless Flow
Beside Walden Creek, Sevier County, Tennessee

This planet seethes with water. Just below
our feet it oozes over, under, through,
around all obstacles, an unseen slough,
a silent sea. Emerging, it will flow
down hillsides, follow ancient beds, and go
on steadily to cleanse, heal, and renew
the earth, conveying life itself unto
all living things. It ambles past us, slow
and humble here, unhurried, ever so
relaxed and easy, as it slithers to
the east of us to make its rendezvous
with other waters, in a ceaseless flow.
Such everywhere abundance whispers of
unfailing faithfulness and steadfast love.

Photons of Thought
Psalm 40.5

The sun feels warm upon my face—I mean,
upon my eyelids, from behind which I
am looking through a wintry, cloudless sky,
expecting not to see, but to be seen.
Photons of thought embrace me, pure, pristine,
life-giving, life-sustaining. Hindered by
no distance, time, or negligence on my
part, they pervade and leave me feeling clean.

Although I do not see their Source, which to
observe directly hardly would be wise,
I know Him by His warming Presence and
bright brilliance, which is just to say, I stand
within His rays and thoughts. No endless skies
nor tight-shut lids can stop His breaking through.

The Little Things

Shaver's Fork, Cheat River, Elkins, WV

The river whispers ceaselessly.
Its murmured message goes unheard
for most of its journey to the sea.

But when at length it passes me
I listen, hoping for a word
of wisdom, or some insight free

of nonsense, pride, or vanity—
some thought I might employ to gird
my mind against mortality.

Its rushing ripples casually
express their views, without a word,
but clearly and convincingly:

"The little things," it says to me,
"done faithfully and well, absurd
as it may seem, combine to be

the bigger things that finally
endure." It is enough for me.

Defiant

The nuthatch feeds defiantly.
He takes his meals head down, you see.
He cares not that some other bird
might find his style a bit absurd,
or that his feeding in this way
exposes him to birds of prey.
Should he, the presence of a hawk
discern, he'll turn around and gawk
unmoving at the sky, as if
to say, by perching still and stiff,
"So find me if you can" (he knows
they tend to focus on what shows
itself alive by movement). Back
again to eating, he will whack
at seeds or insects, some which he
has hidden very carefully
beneath the bark or at some perch,
defying other birds to search
and find his stash. They never do.
He mocks creation's statutes, too,
defying gravity each time
he swallows. He'll cavort and climb
in this position, too, because
he knows that nature's rigid laws
must yield to the defiant mind
which simply will not be supined
by that which others do or say,
but follows on its wonted way
of doing things. His is the duty
defying thus, to teach us beauty.

When Snow Falls

When snow falls, as it is just now,
then I become transfixed somehow.
I stare in wonder and delight
as everything outside turns white.
Amid the falling flakes I seem
to part the veil of some bright dream,
as silence, like a welcome guest,
arrives, and with him, peace and rest.
I try to lock on to one flake
as it descends. What does it take
to craft a thing of such unique
and delicate design? Don't speak
to me of science here; I know
the science of each flake of snow,
and how it forms, and why snowstorms
occur. I understand the norms
and laws. What gives me pause and cause
to wonder, and what frankly awes
me—as that one flake disappears
into the tapestry that cheers
my soul—is pondering the start
of each flake's journey, and its part
in this great work of art which grows
before my eyes, and what it shows
me of the beauty and the power
of Him Whose Word commands this shower
and crafts each crystal masterpiece,
then sets it firmly in the slot or crease
for which it was intended, to
present to my admiring view
this winter wonder. And I see,
in this luxurious gallery,

unseen realities, and all
the cosmos, all things vast and small,
held in their place, fulfilling their
appointed purpose everywhere
according to the One Whose love
snows down upon us from above
so gracefully, though typically
ignored. How callous we can be.

Frail Saplings

Old stump, old archive of a faded past,
your rings reveal the barest hint of lean
and fruitful years. Across your surface green
moss here and there appears, implanted fast
upon the legacy that former years
bequeathed. And in your niches I can see
frail, struggling saplings, like you used to be
so many years ago. Old stump, who hears
your muted witness? Who takes time to heed
your subtle warning, to decode the clues
inscribed upon you, or to learn your views,
discern your wisdom, or embrace your creed?
We stand, the frailest saplings, rooted on
the legacy of generations gone.

Just Doin' Our Job

As if they didn't have enough to do
already—harvesting the light to make
food for the tree and seeing to it you

and I have clean air every day—leaves slake
their host tree's constant thirst by managing
the process whereby unseen roots will take

the water from the soil and, like a spring
of life, disperse it upwards and throughout
the tree, defying gravity—a thing

not easily achieved. But give a shout
out to the leaves, which use osmosis to
accomplish this and keep the tree from drought.

"It's nothing," we leaves say. "We're glad to do
the work each day that we're appointed to."

Logos

The utter regularity of it all!
The summer in its turn gives way to fall,
the fall to winter, spring, and summer; then
the unfailing cycle starts its course again,
the night succumbing to the day, the day
to night. So life to death at last gives way,
albeit suddenly and brutally
at times. As when today, a sparrow's free
unfettered flight was interrupted by
my plate glass door, and he was left to die
in stunned, astonished gasps upon my deck.
I warmed him in my hands, his broken neck
beyond repair, and held him as the light
departed from his eyes and death's cold night
descended. Light to darkness, warmth to cold,
unfailing regularity as old
as being itself. And every sparrow's fall
somehow fulfills a purpose in it all.

Slow Reviving
Shaver's Fork, Cheat River

The fickle rains fell softly through the night,
dropped down upon the trees and trickled down
gnarled grooves of branch and bark to soak the ground
and fill the thirsty conduits out of sight
beneath the forest floor, where they were borne
down hillsides toward the rocky river bed
which lay exposed and parched, like bones long dead,
the day before—smooth stones and boulders, worn
and carried down from the surrounding heights
through untold years of nature's sculpting, lay
unwashed just yesterday, but as the day
plods on, with each arrival of the night's
refreshing rains, they all are baptized in
the river's slow reviving once again.

Whisper of Thunder
Job 26.8-14

The flash and crash were simultaneous.
The whole house shuddered, like it was about
to come apart, and all the lights went out.
The dogs erupted in a frenzied fuss
of frightened yelping, and I ducked my head.
The force of the concussion rocked me to
my soul and shook my body through and through.
I thought a moment that I might be dead.
The strike was just across the street, and set
the neighbor's house on fire. The sudden power
of that fierce lightning bolt caused me to cower—
so close, so inescapable! And yet,
that terrifying crash, that flash and blaze,
they're just the edge and whisper of His ways.

The Ruin of My Sin

*And the fear of you and the dread of you
shall be upon every beast.* Genesis 9.2

He sat, uneasy on a bough, not more
than four short feet from where I had installed
an A-frame hutch, which he had taken for
his nesting-place. I studied him, enthralled
both at his beauty and his industry,
as well as at the cautious way his head
snapped back and forth between his nest and me.
My troubling him thus troubled me. I said,
"Go on now, brother bird; you need not fear
for me. I set that happy house there just
for you and fill your feeders." It was clear,
however, he would offer me no trust.
And so I left him and retired within
to rue once more the ruin of my sin.

Common Brief

I watch the leaves awaken in the wood
behind our home, as daybreak crawls along
the trees, and shafts of sunlight penetrate
the canopy. The leaves are motionless,
but soon enough they'll shake off sleep and dress
for work, which is their God-appointed state.
Though relatively frail, yet they are strong
together as they do the work they should.
I focus on a solitary leaf,
still mostly in the shadows, but intent,
or so it seems, on harvesting the light
within its reach. And thus it lends its might
to join its neighbors, doing what they're bent
to do, as they fulfill their common brief.

Part 4: On Earth as in Heaven

Things Not Seen

Now faith is the assurance of things hoped for, the evidence of things not seen.

Hebrews 11.1

I Heard the Sound of Armies

I heard the sound of armies marching through
the poplar trees, where earth and heaven meet.
The breeze-bent boughs betrayed the unseen feet
of vast, unnumbered hosts, who rushed to do
the bidding of the Lord, beyond the view
of earth-bound men. I knew it was the beat
of countless angels' wings, and rose to greet
them as they passed. O how I wished I knew
their mission! What revolt would they subdue?
What rescue undertake? What mighty feat
essay against dark forces? What complete
and glorious victory would soon ensue?
And then I saw, wind whipping through my hair,
their ranks deployed around me, everywhere.

Curve

It's just a simple curve, gouged by a string
to make a tidy border in between
the walkway and the yard. On one side, green
grass glistens, wearing morning dew like bling.
And on the other side, the walk's the thing.
A simple pleasure, not some glorious scene
replete with soaring mountains, bright blue clean
expansive skies, or oceanscape, or spring
bouquet. No one will ever paint or sing
its charms or mysteries. Simple and pristine,
it speaks to me of verities unseen
but real, which all around us loom and cling
and beckon to horizons far above,
and curve my soul upwards to heavenly love.

Faith

Faith bores into my soul's hard ground
and digs an ever-deepening well
to mysteries I can't fully sound.

Or, like a clapper, faith will pound
against my soul, a waiting bell.
It bores into my soul's hard ground

and rings my soul in rich, profound,
transforming ways. It chimes the spell
of mysteries I can't fully sound.

Faith parts the veil where things abound
unseen, which life's true framework tell.
Faith bores into my soul's hard ground

or strikes soul's mettle to resound
in peals and chimes of heavenly knell,
in mysteries I can't fully sound.

As in a poem lines come around
again, and with new meaning swell,
faith bores into my soul's hard ground
to mysteries I can't fully sound.

Meditations While Reading Ephrem the Syrian[1]

Meditation 1

"Grace has drawn nigh to mouths, once blasphemous,
and has made them harps; sounding praise."

Homily on Our Lord, (1)

Let your speech always be with grace.

Colossians 4.6

Grace wields transforming power. Not even speech
is free from its effects. Diffusing from
a sin-cleansed soul, renewing grace can reach
the world-besotted tongue where it will come
like an invading army on a beach,
to break out and subdue a troublesome
old enemy. Transforming grace knows each
dark redoubt or secluded place where dumb,
vile foes lurk, waiting like a loathsome leech
and clinging to the tongue-ground that has come
into their power. In time, though, grace will teach
the tongue new purposes and skills, the sum
of which no worldly foe can fill the breach
against for very long, but overcome
by thanks and praise and edifying speech,
surrenders all its holdings—all, not some.

---

[1] All quotes are from St. Ephraim the Syrian. *Hymns and Homilies of St. Ephraim the Syrian,* Paul A. Böer, Sr., ed. Veritatis Splendor Publications. Kindle Edition. Scripture quotes are from the *New King James Version.* © Copyright 1982 by Thomas Nelson, Inc. Used by permission. All rights reserved.

Meditation 2

"But our Lord was trampled on by Death; and in His
turn trod out a way over Death."

Homily on Our Lord, (3)

"He will bruise your head, and you will bruise His heel."

Genesis 3.15

No doubt Ol' Nick was smarting still
from that first putdown long ago,
when Jesus blocked his fiendish will
and told him just where he could go.

And after that, for three long years,
the carpenter from Galilee
punched Satan's nose and boxed his ears
and set the demon-harried free.

Nick helpless watched as multitudes
streamed after Jesus and were healed,
and winced to hear them say, "This Dude's
for real!" But he refused to yield.

And then he saw his chance to nail
Him and to show Him who was boss.
He took aim at His heel to whale
Him with a rugged Roman cross.

The blow struck home, and down He went,
but short-lived was the victory,
for three days later Jesus rent

the bonds of death and took that tree

and buried it in Ol' Nick's brain.
Now, though he's wounded mortally
and destined for eternal pain,
he still seeks woe for you and me.

But Jesus has him on a chain
and lets him wander there and here
while He shuts down Nick's vanquished reign
and plunders all his stuff and gear.

So when Ol' Nick comes slinking by
to turn you from the Jesus way,
remember: Every word's a lie
that he suggests or he might say.

So send him packing, lest he know
from you complicity or fruit.
He is a broken, beaten foe,
so just give him the Jesus boot.

Meditation 3

"Thy Word has become a mirror before them, that in it
they might see death, secretly swallowing up their lives."

Homily on Our Lord (5)

*This is a faithful saying and worthy of all acceptance, that Christ
Jesus came into the world to save sinners, of whom I am chief.*

1 Timothy 1.15

Mirror, mirror, of the Word,
who's the foulest, most absurd,
most self-centered, cruel and crude,
most impatient, curt and rude,
most inclined to stray from You
and what You forbid, to do?

Mirror, mirror plainly tell
him who would be marked for hell
but for your long-suffering grace.
Show Him, show the world the face
of the sloth who fails to pray
and consult You every day,
who more likely is to waste
time and energy to taste
idleness's vanities;
more a lazy soul to please
than to know God's filling grace
and to gaze upon His face.

Mirror, mirror, show it true—
he to whom the crown is due

as the chief of sinners! He
whose faint heart You know and see,
he whom death would swallow whole
were it not that You his soul
have redeemed and made Your own,
and throughout Your truth have sown.
Is it the apostle? So
he insisted, but I know
there's another who could claim
this dark honor, this grim fame.

Mirror, mirror, him I see
with heart-rending clarity
as I search Your every line:
That dread title could be mine!

Meditation 4

"Now our Lord bestowed great gifts through small means."

Homily on Our Lord (11)

Therefore, whether you eat or drink, or whatever you do, do all to the glory of God.

1 Corinthians 10.31

For all things are for your sakes, that grace, having spread through the many, may cause thanksgiving to abound to the glory of God.

2 Corinthians 4.15

The glory's in the small stuff, for the small
stuff's never small to whom the glory of
the Lord is known by it—the kindness, love,
encouragement—in short, God's grace, and all
the many small ways Jesus spreads it through
His people to our grace-starved world. A light
and steady rain that goes on day and night
has power to cause the driest desert to
burst forth in life. A daily ray of sunlight
that warms the forest floor can coax unseen
potential to push through, all bright and green
announcing that a new life has begun.
So sweat the small stuff. For where grace prevails
God will be glorified in the details.

Meditation 5

"He was the fisherman Who came down to fish for the lives of the lost."

Homily on Our Lord (15)

"Follow Me, and I will make you fishers of men."

Matthew 4.19

When Jesus came to fish, the only bait
He proffered was His love. They watched Him heal
the sick, feed multitudes, bring down the great
and elevate the lowly, and reveal
the truth of God in words and deeds. He set
His line among a school of unschooled, poor,
unlikely souls. He reeled them in and let
them have a part in His commission, for
He meant them to embrace it as their own.
He kept them—all but one—and though they fled
back to their worldly pools, left Him alone
until at last the Fisherman was dead,
He rose, and gathers them with great increase,
and those once caught, He never will release.

Palimpsest

...written in their hearts... Romans 2.15

We try, but cannot fully scrape away
those ancient words engraved upon the soul.
We would instead compose upon the scroll
of our morality that which today
appeals, although we understand that too
will overwritten be at some point soon
enough. Whatever pleasing, wooing tune
is in the air, whatever views are new
and chic, we write upon our soul, and think
we are at least not out of step with what
the world defines as true and normal. But
we write such codes with disappearing ink.
Meanwhile, those ancient words of love for men
and God persist and will bleed through again.

The Coming of the Kingdom

After Peter Bruegel the Elder's "The Adoration of the Magi in the Snow"

The Kingdom comes like snowflakes, here and there,
in smallest increments, yet steadily.
At first the earth remains unchanged. We see,
however, over time and everywhere,
a Lamb's wool blanket gradually appears,
accumulating on each scar and blight
in pure and pristine coverings of white,
to bring fresh hope and wipe away our tears.

And if we, wondering, ask, "How can this be?"
The Explanation, in the golden mean
of time, lies in a stable rude, by some
adored, by most ignored; but it is He
Whose blood the dark world washes pure and clean
like freshest snow. Thus does His Kingdom come.

Trees in Winter

Denuded, dormant, stark, and spare, the trees
in winter the reviving warmth of spring
await with Stoic beauty. What human being
could stand so bleak and harsh a trial of freeze
and dark and fruitlessness for months on end,
but to emerge all lovely, bursting forth
in bloom and leaf to grace the awakened earth
and cheer the souls of winter-weary men?
And through it all their inner cores grow strong
and broad, their upraised limbs reach for the light,
as if imploring strength with all their might,
while buds form on their branches, all along.
The secret lies within their roots, which hold
their ground and wait amid the bitter cold.

Wear Smooth My Rungs

...ladders against the city... Dallán Forgaill

Wear smooth my rungs by many hands and feet,
O Lord. Let many by my rungs ascend,
Your walls to mount, Your glorious face to greet.

And let me find each clambering burden sweet,
let no complaint arise when I must bend:
wear smooth my rungs by many hands and feet

(complaining thus would not at all be meet
for one created for this very end,
Your walls to mount, Your glorious face to greet).

Some will begin to climb, but then retreat,
yet let me be to all a faithful friend.
Wear smooth my rungs by many hands and feet,

and let no failing on my part defeat
the hopes of those who by my way intend
Your walls to mount, Your glorious face to greet.

Set me on solid ground, let my top beat
against the highest parapets! And then,
wear smooth my rungs by many hands and feet,
who, by me mounting walls, Your face shall greet.

What Job Came to Understand

God dropped down on him, a ferocious Wind
and Weight of Glory, sucked the air out of
his anger and resentment, and in love
laid bare the folly that had seized his mind
and birthed his sin. God drew into the vortex
of His rebuke the vast sweep of creation,
with penetrating questions aimed to station
His Truth immovable within Job's cortex,
affections, and priorities. He blew
away his vain pretense and blew his mind
with mysteries and wonders of the kind
that only God could understand or do.
His brash presumption thus reduced to rubble,
Job found at last the rest he sought in trouble.

Part 5: Mind Training

Four verse essays

While the practice of poetry need not in itself confer wisdom or accumulate knowledge, it ought at least to train the mind in one habit of universal value: that of analyzing the meaning of words...

T. S. Eliot (*The Idea of a Christian Society*)

The Art of Life

"I think the art of life consists in tackling each immediate evil as well as we can." C. S. Lewis

The reality of sin, pervasive and subtle, means that every day is a struggle to maintain and advance the Kingdom of God. Every work, every task, each conversation is an IED waiting to explode in your face, a set of poisonous fangs concealed behind an alluring gaze, the bared talons of a raging eagle, falling frantically toward you. Each moment, though it comes pristine from God, arrives with sharp edges, like broken glass, to cut away your vitality and whittle down your hope. Do not be deceived; no good thing comes naturally or easily. You must be on guard. You must be vigilant. You cannot hide from time's advance or sin's tightening stranglehold. You must fight. You must create. You must redeem each moment and everything in it, washing it in the blood of Christ, polishing it with the grace of the Spirit, and fashioning it on the wheel of the Word to fit the pleasure of God and serve your neighbor. Do not look back, or the accumulation of advancing moments will harden you like a pillar of salt and freeze you in your faithless tracks. Look ahead to where you've been summoned, and craft each opportunity, as it passes through your hands back to Him Who gave it, a journeyman's gift, announcing your soon arrival and tapping into the delight that fills the heart of your awaiting King. To art, then, and life, and without flinching or complaining, for this is your sufficiency each day.

Ray of Dawn

"Thou God of truth Whose certain laws direct
The starry spheres, whilst all the powers above
Admire and tremble; the projected Earth
Rolling along its planetary path
Hath learned to hail Thy triumph; and this age
Enables mortal eyes in Thy great works
To view Thee nearer, and with nobler thought."[2]

So wrote an English vicar to extol
the glory, wonder, beauty, pow'r, and truth
of God, Who showed Himself in one brief ray
of sun, cast through a telescope upon
that vicar's wall, as one small planet in
our solar system made its rare but sure
and hitherto unseen conjunction with
the sun. For Jeremiah Horrox, this
the culmination was of many years
of study, observation, careful thought,
and calculation, as he gave himself
to God and to astronomy, that he
might "trace the stars whose order proves them Thine."

While yet at Cambridge, working to become
a priest, he first began his studies in

---

[2] The primary source for this essay is Arundell Blount Whatton. *Memoir of the life and labors of the rev. Jeremiah Horrox; to which is appended a tr. of his discourse upon the transit of Venus across the sun*. Kindle Edition. Unless otherwise indicated, all quotations are from the works of Jeremiah Horrox. Except for Horrox' poetry, all quotes are edited to fit the constraints of the blank verse form of this essay.

astronomy, entirely on his own.
No course of study then existed in
his native land, and there was not then an
observatory anywhere throughout
all England. So he turned to books. Moved by
all things sublime, and naturally inclined
to speculation, he took great delight
in contemplating all the works of God
that pleased him and that activated his
quick mind. The stars, the planets and the sun,
the moon, and other shining lights high in
the heavens captured his attention. He
desired to learn as much of them as he
could on his own. "It seemed to me," he wrote
"that nothing could be nobler than [to give
myself] to contemplate the wisdom of
my great Creator, as displayed amidst
such glorious works." He longed "to feed upon
their beauty" and "to know their causes" by
more careful observation of them all.

The obstacles were many. Books were hard
to come by, and he had no mentor, no
one to encourage him or help. And he
was poor. He was dispirited at first,
and by the weariness and languor which
the work provoked. He wrote, "What then was to
be done? I could not make the [enterprise]
be easy, or increase my fortune, and
the least of all, encourage others with
a love for astronomic studies. Yet
complaining of philosophy because
it is so difficult is foolish and
unworthy. I determined, therefore, that

the tedium of study should be by
much labor overcome; my poverty,
by patience; and instead of one to teach
me, I would turn to books…For me, it was
a pleasure meditating on the fame
of these great scientific masters, and
to emulate them in my work."

                                    It was
the early 1600s, just before
the dawn of science's new day. And though
he was a priest, with all the duties that
entailed, he studied diligently, and
began to write about his findings. He
wrote several learnèd dissertations and
some tracts—though none was published—to point out
the errors in contemporary thought
regarding matters astronomic. Soon,
his observations led him to improve
the thinking about lunar theory. He
identified the orbit of the moon
around the earth as an ellipse; he was
the first to make this observation. And
in doing so, he set the basis for
Sir Isaac Newton's work on gravity.

For Jeremiah Horrox, details were
his aim, to understand the workings of
the cosmos. He was not content to know
the theological account of all
that is; as far as observation would
allow, and reading, he determined to
explain the ways of God within the vast
creation. As he wrote, "It is most true

that God's will is the cause of everything;
but resting in such generalities
will mean the death of all philosophy."
The Scriptures set the framework and showed how
to think about the cosmos, Horrox thought.
But both books—Scripture and creation—are
essential for obtaining as complete
an understanding of our God and all
His ways as He is pleased to grant to us.
His work paid off. His studies of the moon
alone, wrote his biographer, "suffice
to give him a secure and lasting place
and reputation." Horrox turned his mind
to learn of comets also; and he was
the first to undertake a study of
the ways of tides.

                  But most important for
the course of science were his studies on
the transit of the sun by Venus. He
predicted it for 1639,
though other eminent astronomers
like Kepler favored 1631.

The transit of the sun by Venus comes
when that small planet crosses the sun's face
such that it can be seen from earth. No one
had ever witnessed the event, and none
predicted it till Horrox. It cannot,
of course, be viewed directly. Horrox planned
an indirect approach, committing this
and all his work to God. He wrote, "May He,
the God of all astronomy, and the
Conservator of every useful art,

bless my unworthy efforts for the sake
of His eternal glory and His Name,
and for mankind as well."

                    His plan involved
a dark room with a smallish window, through
which he would aim his telescope to catch
a single ray of sunlight. On the wall,
he placed a circle, in diameter
six inches, which he marked off, like a clock—
360 minutes—which he then
divided further into segments, to
plot Venus' progress once it had appeared.

On Sunday, 24 November, in
the year of our Lord 1639,
he set his telescope to catch a ray
of sun and have it strike his diagram
a perpendicular. Then off he went
to carry out pastoral duties (it
was Sunday, after all). As often as
he could, he checked the diagram, intent
on noticing when any dark, round spot
might enter at the lower left-hand side.
We can imagine the excitement he
was feeling, and especially since he was
at once engaged in all the work that gave
him joy and satisfaction – ministry
and astronomic observation. We
can feel his joy as he expressed it in
the paper he prepared as his report
of this event. He wrote therein, "O God,
profound Divine, how wisely have all Your
decrees arranged the purposes of their

creation! You have given honor to
the patron of all learning; meanwhile, I
have chosen for my theme the Queen of love,
veiled by the shade of Phoebes' light." He praised
God for his telescope, and wrote in verse:
"With daring gaze it penetrates the veil
Which shrouds the mighty ruler of the skies,
And searches all his secret laws. O! power
Alone that rivalest Promethean deeds!
Lo, the sure guide to truth's ingenuous sons!
Wherever the zeal of youth shall scan the heavens,
O may they cherish thee above the blind
Conceits of men, and the wild sea of error
Learning the marvels of this mighty Tube!"

On Saturday, the 23rd, he set
up all his apparatus and began
his observations. He predicted that
the next day Venus would her transit make,
and cast her shadow on the wall within
the diagram which he had set there. But
he wanted to be sure, so he began
to look the day before. Come Sunday, he
would have to check the diagram between
his other obligations. Horrox tells
us what he saw at last: "At 3:15
that afternoon, when I again was free
my labors to continue, all the clouds,
as if by some divine imposing, were
entirely dispersed, and I resumed
my observations. It was then that I
beheld a most delightful spectacle,
the object of my sanguine wishes; for
a spot of no small magnitude, in shape,

a perfect circle, entered on the sun's
disc at the left, so that the limbs of both
the sun and Venus came together as
they should, precisely. Knowing this spot was
the shadow of the planet, I applied
myself to sedulously view it." It
remained in view for thirty minutes, more
or less. But Horrox marked down what he saw,
then wrote, "I was enabled to make all
my observations, though the time was short,
by Providence alone; and they were so
complete, I scarcely could have wished a more
extended time."

     He had arranged to have
a friend named William Crabtree, carry out
the observation also, from his home
in Broughton, so that he might validate
the transit from another site. And this
he did, he said, "in contemplation rapt
and motionless, just barely trusting my
own senses, through excess of joy." In his
report, besides his measurements and all
his viewings, Horrox wrote these words in verse:
"But a sublimer throne is thine, and awe
Ineffable awaits thy lightning's course,
Thou God of truth whose certain laws direct
The starry spheres, whilst all the powers above
Admire and tremble; the projected Earth
Rolling along its planetary path
Hath learned to hail thy triumph; and this age
Enables mortal eyes in thy great works
To view thee nearer, and with nobler thought
To trace the stars whose order proves them thine.

In vain the Sun his fiery steeds would urge,
In vain restrain them, or attempt to guide
Their rapid course within the laws of fate.
The Earth performs their task, and by each day's
Revolving saves to all the distant stars
The useless labor of unceasing motion."

These observations mark the apex of
the scientific work of Horrox. But
he made, besides these, many lasting marks
on the development of science, like
a ray of sun announcing dawn's new day.
He was the first one to discover that
the moon made an ellipse around the earth.
His work led to the understanding of
what came to be described as gravity.
Sir Isaac Newton wrote that Horrox was
most instrumental in transforming what
was then called natural philosophy
from mere fictitious speculation to
the diligent investigation of
the facts of God's creation. Horrox' work
improved our understanding of the tides,
corrected astronomic tables, gave
us insight into comets, and much more,
and all of this while also serving God,
fulfilling all his duties as a priest.

He was a ray of scientific dawn,
and died when he was twenty-two years old.

Looking Up
Solzhenitsyn at Harvard

The prophet scorned the academic dress
of those who had invited him to their
Parnassus of the Ivy League. Why wear
their garb, when he intended not to bless

them, but to warn, and even to condemn
their way of life, their stewardship, their views
and their pretensions? Though he would refuse
their outward show, he would reveal to them

the secrets of their souls, and scorch them by
his unexpected and unwelcome theme.
Dressed in his olive jacket, he might seem
to them a kindred spirit, come to ply

them with some words of revolution, or
congratulations for a job well done.
But what the exile had to say, not one
of them expected, or had answer for.

He spoke about the world that they had made,
about its disregard of history,
its dedication to the urgency
of gaining more and more; the homage paid

to individual rights at the expense
of proven standards of morality.
He chided them, and said they could not see
that they no different were from those against

whom they presumed to stand. He said the world
was split apart, but not politically
(as everyone who heard him thought that he
might say). To their amazement, he unfurled

a different kind of world-split. On the one
hand, those who struggled for the rights of man
(as they regarded them), who had a plan
for mundane happiness, to be hard won

by politics and economics and,
if necessary, military might—
a vision of a world where every right
was granted, everyone could take his stand

on his own chosen ground, and do what he
preferred, within the bounds of law, of course.
The captive East, he argued, was no worse
or better than the West might seem to be.

Their vision was the same, although their means
diverged in many ways. Each sought to make
the most of present moments, and to take
advantage of the other, stealing scenes,

dispatching armies here and there, and when
they could, securing gains and trumpeting
their victories. Their split was not the thing
he wanted to impress on them, not then,

though he had written on that split before;
and, when they read the topic he proposed,
his high-born hosts can only have supposed
that this would be his chosen theme once more.

But it was not. The split he spoke about
was not quite *au courant* within the halls
of academe, amid the ivy walls
of Harvard's hallowed ground. But with no doubt

or hesitation, he pursued his theme:
The world had, in its vanity and pride,
detached itself from God, set Him aside,
and chosen to pursue a foolish dream

of independence from the will of God.
In East and West alike, the interests of
prosperity and power rose high above
all other matters. Socialism trod

down people in the East, while in the West
a loss of will to stand for truth and right
was leaving freedom captive to a night
of deepening despair, from which the best

thoughts even of the brightest men would not
be able to deliver us. For we
had turned away from God's morality
to seek one of our own. And we forgot

that all our rights and freedoms came to us
because we are His image-bearers. Now,
flush with the rights of man, we know not how
to live, nor whom to love, nor what to trust.

No God restrains our passions now; but more
than ever, self-restraint is our great need.
Yet neither our best efforts nor our creed
of self-reliance can our hope restore.

Can we not see that drinking from the cup of mere autonomy and passion would destroy us? Let us therefore do the good and right thing and return to looking up.[3]

---

[3] Aleksandr I. Solzhenitsyn, "A World Split Apart," in *East & West* (New York: Harper and Row, 1980), pp. 39ff.

Music to Part the Veil

On first hearing Mendelssohn's 5th forty years ago.

The winter sun had just begun to light
the morning sky as I cranked up my car
to head back home. The group of men I met
with every Tuesday morning were as bright
as any men I'd ever known. They let
me lead their study, though they held it far
from where I lived, and it was always night

as I was coming out. The radio—
our local classics advocate, not that I knew
that much about such music, but I sought
to—had spun up a piece I did not know,
one filled with gloomy trepidation, fraught
with angst. I thought, This must be leading to
some big symphonic narrative. And so

I tried to pay attention as I drove
into the waking sun. Toward the end,
the tumult settled and resolved into
what seemed a frail "Amen". But then it strove
for just a few more bars. I had no clue
where this was going, what it might portend,
or what was coming next. Just then, it dove

into a lilting rhythm, like a dance
or celebration of some sort. That's weird,
I thought, to follow such uncertainty
with revelry. I felt my fingers prance
upon the steering wheel. I seemed to be
caught up in all this merriment and cheered
out loud and danced as best I could. What chance

this would continue? So I mused. And I
was right, for next a melancholy mood
took over from the dance and seemed to mock
or to curtail its revelry. The sky
was growing lighter now, as if to block
the sullen mood and all the attitude
of gloom it conjured, like a heaving sigh

of resignation heading toward despair.
The music swelled, a great widespread lament,
then settled back to loneliness again.
A fatalistic feeling filled the air,
as when the fondest hopes of desperate men
are dashed. The movement groaned with discontent,
and hopelessness abounded everywhere.

And then, without a pause, the gloom played out,
and underneath it came a solo sound,
a flute—or so I thought. And wait! I knew
that tune: "Ein Feste Burg." Was this about
to be a thing? Oh yes, it was. Then, two
wind instruments as one became firm bound,
and me? I felt as if I just might shout

out "Hallelujah!" any second. More
and more the music swelled in fugues and rounds,
assertive, confident, and bold as all
the instruments unleashed their brightest store
of melody, a rousing, glorious call
to arms! The more those old familiar sounds
compounded, growing sweeter than before,

the more I felt myself caught up within
the flow of something supernatural. I

was driving, but I wasn't. I was being
swept up within the music's current, in
a rapture that was full of joy and freeing
me from my earthly confines to some high
and holy site. The music was a thin

place for my soul, and underneath my feet
the current of the Living Water urges
me forward, upward to that radiant Mount,
from which bright rays abound, and singing, sweet
and awesome, pours forth as if from some fount.
"A...might-y...Fortress..." fills my brain and surges
throughout my soul! I raise my eyes to meet

the radiant Mount, my soul upwelling and
my right hand stretching forward as if I
could reach into the light...and then I know
it's but the morning sun, which through a stand
of trees had broken with a sudden show
of light, illuminating all the sky
and spreading out to wake the sleeping land.

As Mendelssohn's fifth symphony achieved
its summit and came to its rest upon
"His Kingdom is forever!" (or so I
imagined), I was filled with joy, relieved,
and close to tears. And then the morning sky
was bright. My glimpse beyond the veil was gone,
at least for then; and yet those moments cleaved

unto my soul, and I was stretched somehow.
I gave to God abundant thanks and praise
for music that transports me through the veil,
such music as can make me glad to bow

my heart's knee and surmount the earth-bound pale
of my existence, to exalt my gaze
to there and then in all my here and now.

Part 6: Remaining Time

Endings and Beginnings

A bad death never follows a good life: for there is nothing that maketh death bad but that estate that followeth death. Therefore let not their care that needs must die be employed upon the manner of their death, but upon the estate they are eternally to inherit after death...What power hath the horror of any kind of death to affright their souls that have led a virtuous life?

Augustine (*City of God*)

The Mourners

The tragedy of death does not escape
the beasts. This morning, near the stream that flows
this time of year, a neighbor's cow the throes
of death endured, succumbing to her fate
while giving birth. Her calf, still wrapped within
the birth sac, never drew first breath, but lay
beside its wasted mother as the day
broke clear and warm. To the onlooking crows' chagrin,
the farmer came and with his backhoe laid
the stricken mother and her still-born seed
beneath the earth. No grieving, and no need
for ceremony; no respects were paid.
This afternoon three somber mourners made
their way to paw the ground where they were laid.

The Dying
We all fade as a leaf... Isaiah 64.6

It's getting to be time again when all
the leaves, their labors nearly done, prepare
their legacy. We see them everywhere
at work on this, the brilliant hues of fall
announcing the new terms of each leaf's call.
And soon the trees will cast them off to spare
their limbs and branches winter's wear and tear,
and leave the scattered leaves in cold death's thrall.

And yet we love this dying. And we take
for granted the endowment it provides:
fresh fodder to enrich the soil, the earth.
For leaves give back what they consumed, and make
a better world. And so, as each leaf glides
in dying, it fulfills its holy worth.

Years of Strength
Psalm 90.10-12

I'm more aware of time in these my years
of strength. It seems to go much faster now.
I try to use it wisely, but somehow
I never have enough, and it appears
to speed up in inverse proportion to
my slowing down. Thus, many projects I
have planned or have begun will likely die
when I do, in due course. How should I view
these cherished goals? Should I pursue them still
or set my sights on lower fruit? Teach me,
O Lord, to number well this time, to be
a faithful steward and to do Your will.
It's not my time but Yours, Lord. Help me live
for You the moments You are pleased to give.

Hourglass
Psalm 71.9

Each day I wake up, and I swear,
my veins are filled with sand. I sit
a few stunned moments, and I hear

it shifting—over, downward, bit
and grain by bit and grain, as though
my body had been retrofit

by night, while I was sleeping, so
that I am changed from flesh to glass,
made brittle, and I seem to know

my feet and legs are heavy as
a concrete block; and yet my head
feels emptier, lighter than it was

the day before. I might be dead?
I like to think I'm in the prime
of life, and yet I know instead

I'm getting old, that's all, and I'm
just feeling my remaining time.

Tents
2 Corinthians 5.1-11

Fret not that you must one day lay aside
this mortal tent. These bones, this flesh, and all
their fleeting joys shall surely wither, fall,
and turn to dust, no matter how you've cried
or groaned. Life's changeless, fast-receding tide
will carry you out with the great and small
alike, and nothing, nothing can forestall
its force. Groan not that you may here abide.

But groan indeed, and long that you may be
clothed with unfading glory, wrapped about
and bundled up in Him Who, crowned with love,
exudes eternal splendor, majesty,
and might, and Who by grace has marked us out
to dwell forever in His tent above.

Above All Regret

I guess I'll never traipse through snow soft woods
and fields I call my own, to feel the quiet,
and know the lovely loneliness of God's

scarce-sin-touched glory. And I guess the night
sky will remain a mystery to me—all
those ancient lamps and blinking, beckoning lights.

And what chance is there that I'll learn the call
of every local bird? Or know the name
of every plant and tree, the very small

up to the very great? I guess the same
is true for many other things my mind
delights to contemplate. But I'm to blame,

and no one else. I live so far behind
what I imagine; things I'd like to do
or learn just drift away before I find

the time or inclination to pursue
them. But the hankering lingers, and the sad
regret of time and wealth that slipped right through

my careless, thoughtless fingers. It's too bad,
too bad. But all this pointless thinking of
those things I might have learned or done or had

resolves in gratitude for what above
all these is mine: Your love. Your wondrous love.

And When I Die

And when I die, it will no ending be,
but just a passing through the veil that I
have often groped to part. Released from my
now worn-out flesh, from its corruptions free
at last, my soul into eternity
will enter, lifted and escorted by
that holy angel, who at all times my
companion and protector is. And he
will sing a soft and joyous melody,
and I will know it, and be glad as my
soul joins the song, which swells, as from the sky
crescendoing, to cheer and welcome me.
And then, beyond the grip of time and space,
I'll understand the mystery of grace.

April Snow

It snowed all day, for twelve straight hours,
like Winter, brandishing its powers
and letting everybody know
who's boss. At times the snow was so
thick, I could barely see the trees
out my back door. It didn't ease
off 'til an hour or so ago,
and then it stopped. And all that snow
was gone without a hint or trace.
The wintry storm could not erase
the warmth stored up within the ground,
and though it blustered all around
for one entire April day,
when finally it had had its say,
the jonquils shook it off, the green
grass sported a more brilliant sheen,
the buds resumed their swelling on
the tree limbs, and the Old Man, gone
and spent, looked back and shrugged. There is
a time for everything, and his
was at its end for now. But oh,
how lovely was that April snow!

Never Too Late

It's never too late not to waste your life.
Regret is neither vision, goal, nor plan,
so press on, stay the course, endure the strife.

There's no use waiting for some drum and fife
to rally you to action. Be a man!
It's never too late not to waste your life.

So everything you've tried so far is rife
with disappointment—still, believe you can!
And press on, stay the course, endure the strife.

Does this rebuke cut deep, like some dull knife
sheathed in your ego? Take that blade in hand—
it's never too late not to waste your life—

and carve a new direction, slice by slice.
You can't go backwards, and you must not stand
still: press on, stay the course, endure the strife.

Look up, take heart, don't act like a naïf;
run, run each day to gain the promised land!
It's never too late not to waste your life,
so press on, stay the course, endure the strife.

Offering
Diademata

Take then these off'rings, Lord,
in Spirit wrought for You,
composed to magnify Your Word,
so upright and so true!
Let not my sins obscure
these gifts I gladly give,
but let my stains be white and pure
that these with You may live.

Sanctify every word
composed with threads of love;
according to your two-edged Sword
fit them for heav'n above!
These works of hands and soul,
which humbly here I raise,
receive with them, each one and whole,
my heartfelt thanks and praise!

Acknowledgements

"A Curious Contingency" in *BooksandCulture.com*, April 2003

"The Spark of Art and Spirit" in *Theology Today*, Volume 62, Number 1, April 2005

"Fault Lines" in *The Formalist*, Volume 14, Issue 1, 2003

"Logos" in *Theology Today*, Volume 59, Number 4, January 2003

"Ambassadors of Glory" in *Consider the Lilies* (Phillipsburg: P & R, 2005)

"Slow Reviving" in *Preparing Your Church for Revival* (Ross-shire: Christian Focus, 2001)

"The Ruin of My Sin" in *Theology Today*, Volume 59, Number 4, January 2003

"I Heard the Sound of Armies Marching" in *The Formalist*, Volume 11, Issue 2, 2000

"She Lay Beside Me" in *The Formalist*, Volume 10, Issue 2, 1999

"Photons of Thought" in *The Reformed Journal*, November 22, 2022.

Special thanks to Evan Mantyk and The Society of Classical Poets for publishing the following:

"Poetry"
"In Two Minds"
"Pollinator"
"My World"
"Enough!"
"Baking Day"
"Desuetude"
"Gray"
"Centaury"

"When Snow Falls"
"Common Brief"
"Curve"
"Meditations"
"Palimpsest"
"The Dying"

www.ingramcontent.com/pod-product-compliance
Lightning Source LLC
LaVergne TN
LVHW051649080426
835511LV00016B/2573